*Are you ready for*
# CHRISTMAS?

# Are you ready for
# CHRISTMAS?

Roger
Carswell

**10 Publishing**
a division of 10 of those.com

Copyright © 2016 by Roger Carswell

First published in Great Britain in 2016

The right of Roger Carswell to be identified as the Author of this Work has been asserted by him in accordance with the Copyright, Designs and Patents Act 1988.

British Library Cataloguing in Publication Data
A record for this book is available from the British Library

ISBN: 978-1-910587-82-9

Designed and typeset by Pete Barnsley (CreativeHoot)

Printed in Denmark by Nørhaven

10Publishing, a division of 10ofthose.com
Unit C, Tomlinson Road, Leyland, PR25 2DY, England

Email: info@10ofthose.com
Website: www.10ofthose.com

This book is dedicated to the displaced people of Europe and the Middle East. We are well aware of the tragedy of your situation and your terrible plight. We feel deeply for your loss and pain, and want you to know that you are not forgotten, especially at this time of year. May the age-old Christmas message bring you new hope and peace.

# CONTENTS

# INTRODUCTION

When I was growing up, Christmases seemed years apart; now they appear to have just a few months between them. Christmas never seems too far away. There are even Christmas shops open all-year round! Like a microwave meal for one, Christmas is here in no time.

At the end of each August the first signs of Christmas appear in the department stores. By the time September is over Christmas music is being piped at us, an early Christmas card arrives in our post and soon after town and city Christmas lights are switched on by someone given 'celebrity' status. It is then time for us to rummage in some cubbyhole to find last year's decorations, either using or discarding the old Christmas tree, and we begin dreaming of the very elusive white Christmas.

The first twenty-four days of December rush by, with the atmospheric church carol service providing almost the only hour to sit and reflect. We know Christmas Day is very near when we are asked, 'Are you ready for Christmas?' We go over the preparations. Is the food ordered? Are *all* the presents bought and wrapped? Have the Christmas cards been posted to *all* our relatives? Are *all* the guests invited for Christmas dinner? Have the games been organised? Is there enough food to see us over until the shops open next? Am I ready for Christmas? Have I forgotten something?

Once, a mother and father were having a gathering to mark the birth of their newborn child. All the guests were welcomed and had a great time celebrating, eating and drinking. After a while, though, one of the ladies said, 'Well, bring the baby out. Let's see him.' The mother went to the crib, but the baby was nowhere to be seen. Overcome with fear, she panicked. Suddenly she remembered that the baby was still at her parents' house where she had left him that morning! In enjoying the celebration the guests had forgotten who it was all about.

On another occasion a surly teenager was asked whether he had received everything he wanted for Christmas. 'No, I didn't get everything I wanted,' he mumbled, adding, 'But then it's not my birthday, is it?' We get so wrapped up in what the shops have to sell us that we can easily miss who Christmas is all about.

From almost the beginning of time God was getting the world ready for the first Christmas. The Bible tells us that when our first ancestors disobeyed God and introduced sin and death into the world, God distinctly promised that a day would come when the seed or offspring of a woman would destroy the work of the devil himself.[1] In the very phrasing of that initial promise is the beginning of a mystery that would become clear centuries later.

As the Bible unfolds more information is given as to exactly how this pledge would be fulfilled. We read of prophets foretelling that the promised child would be born of a virgin. More wonderfully, He would be God Himself come to earth clothed in humanity. This Son of God would be the 'Wonderful Counsellor, Mighty God, Everlasting Father, Prince of Peace'. Jesus Christ would be born in Bethlehem, then taken to Egypt before growing up in Nazareth.[2] God would take on Himself humanity. The greatest gift of Christmas would be that God would give Himself.

Shepherds on the hills near Bethlehem were made ready to celebrate that first Christmas when angels told them, 'For there is born to you this day ... a Saviour, who is Christ the Lord.'[3] They went quickly, leaving their sheep, to visit the baby. Wise men from the East were ready for that Christmas too as they followed the star which led them to worship the King of the Jews.[4] Today God is also helping us get ready to worship His Son, Jesus the King.

Jesus came to earth to save us from ourselves, our sin, our enslavement to Satan and rebellion against God, and our separation from God. The baby who was laid in a wooden crib would eventually be laid on a wooden cross. There He would suffer as He took on Himself the sins of the world. God's love is such that He sent Jesus to pay the price of our wrong, taking the punishment we deserve. He died that we might be forgiven and brought to know God as our loving Father. As a baby, Jesus was in a virgin womb for nine months. After His death He was laid in a virgin tomb for three days, but then He defeated death and rose again.

Today, because of what Jesus has accomplished for us on the cross, God wants us to turn from our own rebellious ways, where we seek to ignore or reject Him. Instead He yearns for us to ask Him to forgive us, and then He will bring us to know Him. As we trust Jesus and all He has achieved for us, we find we need not fear death or hell. We can know we are God's beloved children for all eternity. Asking Jesus to become your Lord and Saviour is the best way to be ready for Christmas … and the New Year … and all the future!

You never know the true joy of Christmas until you look to God and tell Him that you have received His gift to you. This little book explains what that means and how you can really be ready for Christmas.

# CHRISTMAS IS SPECIAL – GET READY!

*O holy night! The stars are brightly shining,*

*It is the night of our dear Saviour's birth.*

*Long lay the world in sin and error, pining*

*'Til He appeared and the soul felt its worth.*

*A thrill of hope, the weary world rejoices,*

*For yonder breaks a new and glorious morn.*

> *Fall on your knees! O hear the angel voices!*
>
> *O night divine, O night when Christ was born;*
>
> *O night, O holy night, O night divine!*

*Adolphe Adam* [5]

There is a joke about a gangster who forced his way into a flat with the intention of killing a husband and wife.

Pointing his gun at the terrified wife, the gangster asked, 'What's your name?'

She replied, 'Ruth'.

To this the gangster retorted, 'Ah, I can't kill you; my mother was called Ruth'.

He turned to the husband and demanded his name. The desperate man stuttered, 'S-S-S-Simon, but all my friends call me Ruth!'

Names are always important. Parents carefully choose appropriate names for their children. We have clues about a person's ancestry by surnames such as Butcher, Thatcher or Smith. People's names in Bible days in the Middle East were particularly significant. They were used to convey messages as well as reflect character. In the Bible there are more names for Jesus than there are days in a year. Those names tell us why Christmas is so important and how it should mean more than simply a few days of family time away from work. He is called 'Jesus', which means 'Saviour'; and 'Immanuel', which means 'God with us'; and 'Christ', which means 'the Messiah' who had been prophesied for centuries.

Who Jesus is gives us the reason why, over 2000 years after His birth, people all over the world celebrate His birthday. It may be that His actual birthday was not December 25th, but the commemorating of this baby is universal and unique. While we may know the birthday of some of history's greatest characters, such as Sir Winston Churchill or Neil Armstrong, I do not know anyone who commemorates them today. Yet the birth of this baby in a manger still causes the shops to shut and the world to sing His praise and celebrate. Indeed, He is the 'Prince of Peace' and most people would love more peace in our day.

In 1914 Jesus' birth brought about an unforgettable day of peace in the midst of war. It was to become one of history's most famous football matches. A few months earlier World War I had erupted and the fierce fighting had already claimed nearly a million lives. But around Christmas a series of unofficial ceasefires occurred along the Western Front. Despite the cold, frosty conditions, German soldiers began singing, 'Silent night, holy night', then soldiers from both German and English sides ventured into no man's land, where they exchanged food and souvenirs, and eventually played football games together! Hours later the killing continued, but Jesus' birth certainly made its impact. My family still treasures a gift given by a German soldier to my grandfather-in-law after that football match. This incident also continues to be remembered. For example, Sainsbury's used it as their Christmas advertisement theme in 2014.

Surrounding the birth of Jesus was not only a heavenly host, but also a host of words we love and would delight in seeing realised today. The angel who appeared to the shepherds proclaimed news of 'joy', as the long-hoped-for Saviour and Christ had been born.[6] Then the heavenly host who appeared with him proclaimed a time of 'peace'.[7]

Joy, hope and peace are part of the Christmas story, but they are absent from the reality of some people's lives. Some time after Jesus' birth King Herod ordered the killing of all baby boys in the Bethlehem area because He felt threatened by the newborn king.[8] Today, all these years later, hostility towards Jesus remains a current political issue: followers of Jesus in several parts of the world are persecuted and killed, and the media in the West – as well as those in the celebrity elite – love to indulge their hatred of Jesus.

When Field Marshal Lord Montgomery was

asked on *Desert Island Discs* which book he would choose to take with him if marooned on an island, he replied that he would take his own book, one entitled *The History of Warfare*, and would devote his time to pondering how he could stop people from fighting. Yet that is exactly what Jesus came to do. He came to bring peace. We crave peace and the 'Prince of Peace' is God's gift to meet the longing we have.

God, who is infinitely loving *and* totally just, by nature could never be guilty of hatred or hostility. He remains holy, true and pure. It is we who have gone our own way, daring to defy God by ignoring all that He has for us. We have decided that 'We don't do God!' And yet, as the Bible says of God, 'the Father has sent the Son as Saviour of the world.'[9] God did not send to earth a politician to broker peace, nor a paid mediator to negotiate a compromise, but His own Son. God made this sacrifice because His desire is that we might know Him.

If our greatest need had been information, God would have sent us an educator. If our greatest need had been technology, God would have sent us a scientist. If our greatest need had been possessions, God would have sent us an economist. If our greatest need had been pleasure, God would have sent us an entertainer. But our greatest need is forgiveness, so God sent us a Saviour. Jesus was not merely a religious leader, a great teacher or a miracle worker. He is more than a fine example who cared for the underdog. He is the Saviour of the world.

Throughout history when God has wanted to get the attention of the world, His solution has often been to send a baby. When God's people were living in slavery in Egypt, crying out for a deliverer, God sent the baby Moses, the Prince of Egypt, who in time was to lead the Israelites towards their promised land. Centuries later, when the nation was crumbling, God sent the baby Samuel who was to lead them to better days. Christmas is about God sending a very special baby, and with Him the means for people to be brought into a relationship with Himself.

# GOD PREPARED
# THE WORLD FOR THE
# FIRST CHRISTMAS

*For lo! the days are hastening on*

*By prophet-bards foretold,*

*When with the ever-circling years*

*Comes round the age of gold;*

*When peace shall over all the earth*

*Its ancient splendours fling,*

*And the whole world send back the song*

*Which now the angels sing.*

Edmund Hamilton Sears [10]

One Christmas cartoon showed a little boy gazing into a shop window, which had a sign saying, 'Have the best Christmas ever!' The boy thoughtfully remarked, 'It's pretty hard to beat the first one!' Yet we try our best to do so. Christmas markets, lights, trees, presents and cards create a magical atmosphere. The beautiful but hot town of Glendale in California even blows machine-manufactured snow over the central square throughout the Christmas season. We plan to make each Christmas as special and memorable as possible, especially for children. Christmas Day is pivotal in our calendar.

The events surrounding the first Christmas, which witnessed the birth of Jesus, were totally spectacular. No future monarch or emperor has had his or her birth marked by a star in the sky. Angels announced to working shepherds on the hillside around Bethlehem that a baby had been born, and wise men travelled from the East to worship the infant child. His birth sent shock waves through the palace of Jerusalem, where King Herod reigned. However, consider this intriguing fact: Jesus' biography was written long before He was born.

Early in history, long before His birth, Jesus' coming to earth was announced and anticipated, so that through all the pages of the Bible there is an eager looking forward to His arrival. In the third chapter of the Bible, Genesis 3, immediately after sin had entered the world because of Adam's and Eve's actions, God promised that the 'offspring' of a woman would 'crush' the head of the serpent, Satan.[11] The foretelling of the coming Messiah became clearer as Abraham, Moses, David and then the prophets gave increasing amounts of information about the One who was to come.

The Jews were waiting for this promised Messiah, expecting Him to be a military hero who would deliver them from the Romans. They expected Him to be born in a palace with great pomp. They certainly did not expect Him to lead a life of service, love and humility which would lead to crucifixion.

But Bible prophecies foretold that He would be born in Bethlehem, a 'little town', as we sing in our famous Christmas carol; that His mother would be a virgin; that He would be taken to Egypt; and yet that He would be of the town of Nazareth in the North of Israel.[12] People must have wondered how these prophecies could all be fulfilled in one solitary life. Now we see how they were. They were looking for Someone who would combine the Jewish roles of prophet, priest and king, yet be the Saviour of the world. They were looking for One who would set the people free. Jesus did all of this through His coming to earth, His life, death and resurrection. As the carol 'O Little Town of Bethlehem' proclaims, 'the hopes and fears of all the years are met' together in Jesus at His birth.

Other prophecies concerning the coming Christ predicted the life He would live, the miracles He would perform, the influence He would have and then described in detail His death, even though they were written long before crucifixion was devised as a means of execution.[13] They told us about His resurrection from the dead. Jesus was not just a great religious leader who said and did amazing things that have impacted us for generations, but the long-awaited Messiah who had come to bring His people back to Himself.

Some years ago, a few days before Christmas, I joined a team of people from a Glasgow church who were going on a late-night 'soup run', as they did each Thursday evening. It was a bitterly cold night. We set off at 10 p.m. and visited hostels, people living rough on the streets and under flyovers, as well as those who worked the streets through the night.

We gave them each a hot drink, soup, sandwiches and a Christmas present. A businessman called Wally led the team. For over fifteen years he had not missed a single Thursday night to be involved in the work.

Just after 3 a.m., five hours after setting off, we went to a drunk lying on some grating near a department store. Wally went up to him, gently shook him and said, 'Jock, it's Wally. I have some food for you.' Jock did not respond. Eventually Wally lay on the ground next to Jock, spoke face to face with him, told him that Jesus loves him, gave him some hot chocolate, and put the gift and sandwiches in Jock's overcoat pockets.

To me, what I saw was a thumbnail picture of the Christmas message. God could have ignored us, in much the same way that Wally could have chosen to stay at home each Thursday night. Instead, because of His great love for us, God chose to send His Son to our very scarred world to be harassed and maligned as He met the needs of all whom He encountered, and ultimately to go to His death on a cross and carry on Himself the wrong and rebellion of which we are guilty. Jesus came to earth as the 'Prince of Peace' to give peace. He provides a way for people to experience peace with God and the peace of knowing that God is in control of all things.

Jesus was born in an enemy-occupied country. Hardy shepherds living out in fields near to Bethlehem were keeping watch over their flocks at night. An angel of the Lord appeared to them and said:

> *Do not be afraid, for behold, I bring you good tidings of great joy which will be to all people. For there is born to you this day in the city of David a Saviour, who is Christ the Lord ... And suddenly there was with the angel a multitude of the heavenly host praising God and saying: "Glory to God in the highest, And on earth peace, goodwill toward men!"*[14]

This is the great news that we celebrate. However, we may ask why, if God always keeps His promises, of which there are hundreds in the Bible, where is the peace that God promises here? How is it that 2000 years later war, terrorism, violence, aggression and hatred persist on a global and local scale? Why do outbreaks of peace not last? Over 8000 peace treaties have been made and broken in the last 3100 years, in which only 286 years have been without war. Surely peace has to be more than just a brief moment when people are reloading their weapons?

We long for peace in our minds. Yet no amount of money can ever buy peace. It is not found in a bottle or a pill. Moving house, changing job, finding better friends or even a new spouse will never bring lasting peace. Nor is peace the absence of problems. Instead it is a gift of God, which we can receive from Him.

The mistake millions of people, often deeply religious individuals too, make is trying to achieve peace with God by their *own* efforts. Yet the way to enjoy this has already been achieved by *God*. The thing which keeps us from peace is sin. God says that there is no peace for the wicked. They are like a troubled sea which cannot rest but throws up filth and debris.[15] But peace with God can be found through faith in Jesus Christ and His death on our behalf. God has not left it to us to bring about peace with Him; rather, if we receive Jesus as Lord of our lives, His peace will be given to us. It is a wonderfully unconditional peace – instead of us needing to try to make peace or to work for it, we are simply to enter into the peace which has been purchased for us.

Just as little children can sleep when holding their mother's or father's hand, because they know that they are with someone strong who will protect them, so all those who belong to God can know peace, for they are safe in the arms of Jesus.

My father, a lawyer, used to say, 'Where there's a will, there is a family argument!' Before His death on the cross Jesus gave instructions that in effect were spelling out His will. He asked His disciple John to care for His mother. He committed His spirit to His Father. But earlier to His followers He said, 'Peace I leave with you; my peace I give you.'[16] What a legacy! Jesus, who was always at peace with Himself and with His Father, God, made a will that cannot be set aside by any lawyer, jury or family member. In fact, Jesus rose from the dead to execute the will! If Jesus had left us gold, thieves would have stolen it long ago, but He left to those who believe in Him peace, and no power on earth can take it from those who trust Him.

H.G. Wells, the author of *The War of the Worlds*, wrote, 'Here I am at sixty-four, still seeking peace. It is a hopeless dream.' However, if he had trusted the Jesus who came to bring men and women to God, he would have found both peace with God and the peace of God. Once a person has asked Jesus to become their Lord and Saviour, the enmity between God and them is removed. Moreover, God then fills the person with Himself, by the Holy Spirit, so that whatever situation they face in life, God promises to be with them, giving His peace.

If Christmas shows us anything, it demonstrates that God is not only interested in the world but, in fact, involved in our world. He is not afar, but close to each one of us. The great scientist Sir Isaac Newton said, 'I can take my telescope and look millions of miles into space; but I can go away to my room and in prayer get nearer to God and heaven than I can when assisted by all the telescopes of earth.' He was right. God's desire for us is that we might lay down our arms, turning from our disobedience towards God and instead trusting in Him.

When a person knows that their sin has been forgiven, that they are made right with God, that they are being led and helped through life by Him, and that when they die they are going to be with God in His heavenly home, rather than in the hell they deserve, they can enjoy peace. A Christian knows that all their past has been blotted out, that God is with them every step of life's journey, and that their eternal future is secure because of what Jesus has done for them.

The Bible tells us not only about how as individuals we can enjoy peace with God and the peace of God, but that one day there will be global peace. It is interesting that Bible prophets who foretold the coming of Jesus centuries before He was born also spoke of His coming back to earth to rule as the King of kings and Lord of lords. His reign will be one of peace, justice and righteousness. Everyone who has come to know God through Jesus will be with Him for ever. They will be at peace with themselves and each other because they are at peace with God. Indeed, 'He will judge between the nations and will settle disputes for many peoples. They will beat their swords into ploughshares and their spears into pruning hooks. Nation will not take up sword against nation, nor will they train for war any more.'[17] By being ready to meet the Christ of Christmas, we are actually making ourselves ready for God's plan not only for the next few weeks but for the future of the world.

# GOD CAME DOWN
## AT CHRISTMAS

*He came down to earth from heaven*

*Who is God and Lord of all,*

*And His shelter was a stable*

*And His cradle was a stall.*

*With the poor, and mean, and lowly,*

*Lived on earth our Saviour holy.*

Cecil Frances Alexander [18]

My seventy-two-year-old barber recently retired. He was the type who did not ask what style of haircut you wanted, and certainly not whether you wanted a dye. But he was quick and good, and could always tell you which horse was worth putting some money on! I asked him if he had calculated how many haircuts he had done in his time. He had – 550,000 of them. 'And were any memorable?' I asked. 'Not really,' he replied.

Life is so daily, so routine. But the unusual, even the startling, does sometimes happen. These words, near the beginning of the Gospel of John in the Bible, are stunning: 'There came a man who was sent from God; his name was John …'[19] Pausing our minds to linger on those words would leave us wide-eyed. But actually they are squeezed between something which is even more mind-blowing.

John's Gospel opens with, 'In the beginning was the Word, and the Word was with God, and the Word was God.' It reminds us of the opening words of the Bible: 'In the beginning God created the heavens and the earth.'[20] But now John tells us that Jesus, 'the Word', is this same God and came into our world. God took on human form and lived on earth. Now, that is good news. Another name for Jesus is 'Immanuel', which means 'God with us'. Immanuel became an infant to live among and save us.

On Christmas Eve 1968 astronauts Frank Borman, James Lovell and William Anders emerged in their Apollo 8 spacecraft from behind the moon. They were so impressed by the God who made the planets that a listening world heard them read the opening words of the Bible: 'In the beginning God created the heaven and the earth...' It is worth hearing those immortal words by listening to them via the Internet![21] The same God who made the planets is the One who gave us the first Christmas. The little baby, Jesus, who was born and laid in a manger, was to divide time in two – BC and AD – and bring hope to our world. God chose not to wash His hands of our world, but instead came to rescue us.

Preparing for Christmas often means making travel arrangements and, for those not travelling by car, hoping that the airline employees or railway staff will not call a strike. Christmas is a time for travel; it always has been. Nowadays we travel to be with family or friends. 2000 years ago Mary and Joseph walked the eighty miles from Nazareth, where they lived, to Bethlehem, their ancestral home. They were given no choice about this journey for Caesar

Augustus had made his famous decree that everyone had to return to their place of origin to be registered.[22]

Similarly, after the birth of Jesus, the shepherds travelled from the nearby hills where they had been guarding their sheep to worship the baby Jesus. They went to see Him in His manger in Bethlehem because angels from heaven had announced to them that this baby was the Saviour, Christ the Lord. Likewise, wise men from the East made their way over hundreds of miles, following a star, to give gifts of gold, frankincense and myrrh to Jesus.

More journeys were to follow. Because of King Herod's jealous rage and threats to kill Jesus, Joseph, Mary and their child had to escape as refugees to Egypt, waiting there until Herod died before they could return to Nazareth, where Jesus was to grow up. But the greatest journey of all was Jesus coming from the heart of heaven to live on this earth, and then His journey to the cross at a place called Calvary.

Once an African schoolboy listened as his teacher explained why we give gifts at Christmas. Later, on the final day of term before the Christmas holidays, he presented to her a gift that had been wrapped up. Asking if she could open it then and there, she carefully took off the layers of paper to discover a beautiful shell. She expressed her awe at the gift and asked where the boy had got such a shell. He replied by naming the beach where such shells can be found. Knowing it was a long distance away, she asked how the boy had got there. He replied by saying that he had walked. 'But that is miles away,' she exclaimed. 'The long walk was part of the gift,' he answered.

Jesus coming to earth could not have been a greater journey, but He came because, as God, He had seen the rottenness of the world and the consequences of our human rebellion against our Creator. As human beings, we are all proud and hard-hearted, feeling that we do not need or want God. We are guilty of pushing Him to the edge of our lives. Sometimes we do this defiantly, at other times in a self-righteous way, but it is always wrong.

Isaiah lived 700 years before Jesus but, prophesying His coming, wrote:

*For unto us a Child is born,*

>   *Unto us a Son is given;*

>   *And the government will be upon*
>   *His shoulder.*

>   *And His name will be called*

*Wonderful, Counsellor, Mighty God,*

*Everlasting Father, Prince of Peace.*

*Of the increase of His government*
*and peace*

*There will be no end,*

*Upon the throne of David and over*
*His kingdom,*

*To order it and establish it with judgement*
*and justice*

*From that time forward, even forever.*

*The zeal of the Lord of hosts will*
*perform this.*[23]

God, who is a spirit, clothed Himself in humanity as He entered our world. God was big enough to become small, and strong enough to become as weak as an infinitesimally minute foetus implanted in a virgin mother's womb in Nazareth. Jesus is called 'Mighty God, Everlasting Father'. John describes His remarkable act of condescension as he starts his Gospel: 'In the beginning was the Word, and the Word was with God, and the Word was God … The Word became flesh and made his dwelling among us.'[24] Centuries later the great hymn writer Charles Wesley expressed this wonder in his carol 'Let Earth and Heaven Combine', as, 'Our God contracted to a span, incomprehensibly made man.'

Like two musical chords coming together to make beautiful music, deity and humanity combined in the person of Jesus. He was as much a man as any man is a man, and as much God as God is God! Jesus was fully human and fully divine. He is the physical manifestation of God the Father. Of course, this is beyond what we can really understand, but then if we could fathom the depths of God, that would mean that either He would not be God or we would not be human. Through Jesus, the transcendent, invisible, infinite God drew near to us, making Himself known.

As He was fully human, Jesus knew what it was to be tired, tempted, hungry, thirsty, sad and lonely, but also happy and gregarious. Yet, as He was also fully divine, He had the power to know other people's thoughts; to turn a few loaves and fish into food to feed thousands; to heal the sick and raise the dead; to live a totally sinless life; but then to carry on Himself the sin of the world, giving Himself to death, before three days later rising again.

On one occasion a traditional school nativity play that took place in Barnsley, South Yorkshire, went wrong, but it did illustrate this amazing truth. Parents, aunts, uncles, grandparents and others gathered to watch their nine-year-olds perform. Onto the stage came a Roman soldier, who unfurled a scroll and read out the decree from Caesar Augustus that the world was to be registered. Joseph and Mary, who had several cushions stuffed up her robes, turned and said that they would have to travel to Bethlehem. They began to make their way across the stage followed by their donkey – two boys covered with a brown-grey coloured blanket. So far, so good.

The second scene was set in the stable. Mary and Joseph, who were now beside a manger in which there was a doll, the baby Jesus, were on one side of the stage. On the other side, girls dressed as angels in net curtaining announced to shepherds that a baby had been born in Bethlehem. The shepherds turned to each other saying, 'Let us now go, even unto Bethlehem, and see this thing that the Lord has made known unto us.' Again, everything so far had gone to plan.

All that remained was for the three wise men to come onto the stage. They were wearing dressing gowns and Bacofoil crowns, each carrying a gift of gold or frankincense or myrrh. The first moved across the stage, said his lines and presented his gift to Jesus. The second did the same. But the third, while waiting, had spotted his parents in the audience and, overcome by a sense of awe and occasion, lost his lines. He had sufficient presence of mind to keep moving, but could not recall his words. The teacher whispered in the wings, 'Say something' but there was silence. In desperation, after a long silence, the teacher said, 'Say anything!'

What does a little boy know to say to a baby? He looked into the manger and, with a big, broad Yorkshire accent, said, 'Eh, he's just like his dad!' The crowd laughed, but actually this boy had expressed a great truth. The Bible expresses it somewhat differently, saying of Jesus that, 'He is the image of the invisible God'.[25] Jesus revealed to us what God is like. He spoke, acted and reacted as only God would. And all that He did was motivated by love.

I find it amazing that Jesus, the Son of God, should be willing to be born and laid in a manger; to experience all the challenges of living in a despised northern town of Israel; and to act in humility towards His disciples, even washing their feet, a job which would usually be done by a servant. His favourite title for Himself was 'Son of Man' (which can be found eighty-four times in the Gospels alone) as this reveals His humility yet proclaims His authority.

There are many fundamental differences between Christianity and all other religions, but if Jesus is God, then Jesus as the Creator gave existence itself to Buddha, Muhammad, Confucius and all other religious leaders! Jesus said what only one who is fully God could say:

> *Therefore My Father loves Me, because I lay down My life that I may take it again. No one takes it from Me, but I lay it down of Myself. I have power to lay it down, and I have power to take it again. This command I have received from My Father.*[26]

That is why He came into the arena of human history.

# GOD, MAKING US
# READY FOR HIM

*Sacred Infant, all divine,*

*What a tender love was Thine,*

*Thus to come from highest bliss*

*Down to such a world as this.*

*Hail, thou ever-blessed morn!*

*Hail, redemption's happy dawn!*

*Sing through all Jerusalem,*

*Christ is born in Bethlehem.*

*Edward Caswall* [27]

December 22nd 2009 was a cold night, but nevertheless Prince William slept rough on a street in central London. His motives, no doubt, were to identify with and understand those less fortunate than himself. The royal bedded down in a sleeping bag next to a group of wheelie bins near Blackfriars Bridge to experience being homeless. Of course he was guarded. Apparently the scariest moment came when he was almost run over by a road sweeper. He survived for the well-informed news media to tell the tale.

Jesus came to earth and experienced the joys and sorrows of living on this planet. But as God, He knew all things anyway. He did not come simply to experience humanity; He came to save us.

Joseph was betrothed[28] to be married to Mary. They had not yet come together sexually, but he heard that Mary was expecting a child and felt deeply disturbed, surmising that he had been betrayed by the woman he loved. He concluded that the most honourable course of action was to break up the relationship without making a fuss. But then an angel of the Lord spoke to him. He reassured him not only that Mary had not acted unfaithfully, but that she was to give birth to a child who was miraculously conceived. God even gave the child His name, Jesus, which means Saviour, because He would save His people from their sins. Jesus the Saviour is an apt description of who He is and what He came to do.

Throughout His life Jesus went out of His way to reach out to people who needed 'saving'. Sitting at a well in the village of Sychar, Jesus met a Samaritan woman who had been married and divorced five times and was now living with another man. Jesus demonstrated that He knew all about her past, but explained how He could give her life that would be like water springing up within her, giving her vitality and freshness – spiritual life could be hers. She ran back to her home town and told everyone, 'Come, see a Man who told me all things that I ever did.'[29] She found salvation, and forgiveness for her past, through Jesus.

Hours away from His own crucifixion, Jesus spent time with Zacchaeus, a little man who had bought from the Romans the right to tax his own people. In doing so Zacchaeus exploited them to the extent that they would not even permit him to enter the synagogue to worship. Yet when he heard that Jesus was nearing his town, he so wanted to see Jesus that he scrambled up a sycamore tree to get a view of Him.

Jesus focused on him, called him down, dined with him and totally transformed his life. Jesus Himself testified that salvation had come to Zacchaeus' heart and home. Zacchaeus was transformed to such an extent that he gave back four times what he had taken from anyone he had cheated, plus he gave half of all that he had to the poor.[30]

On another occasion, as Jesus was teaching early one morning in the temple, religious leaders dragged to Him a woman whom they had caught in the act of committing adultery. They wanted her stoned to death. Jesus said, 'He who is without sin among you, let him throw a stone at her first.' The only person there who was without sin was Jesus, who had no desire for her to be stoned to death, so her accusers left the scene. Jesus then asked the woman, 'Has no one condemned you? … Neither do I condemn you; go and sin no more.'[31]

Even when Jesus was being crucified, He saved the dying thief who was being put to death next to Him. This thief, recognising his own sinfulness as his thoughts turned to God, called to Jesus and asked, 'Lord, remember me when You come into Your kingdom.' Jesus replied, 'Assuredly, I say to you, today you will be with Me in Paradise.'[32] When you stop and think, it is clear that heaven will be filled with bad people … who have been forgiven!

But Jesus not only saved people whom He met long ago; He also came to save us from our sins today. He said, 'For God so loved the world that He gave His only begotten Son, that whoever believes in Him should not perish but have everlasting life.'[33] Jesus was born destined to die for us. When He suffered as He was crucified, He carried on Himself the sin of the world. All the wrong of humanity, from the beginning to the end of time, was laid on Him. Isaiah prophesied not only about Jesus' birth, but also about His death. Isaiah 52:13 through to 53:12 describes in detail what would happen when the Messiah died. Handel's famous *Messiah* puts this prophecy to music, particularly the memorable words from Isaiah 53:6: 'All we like sheep have gone astray; We have turned, every one, to his own way; And the LORD has laid on Him [Jesus] the iniquity [evil deeds] of us all.'

I once saw a cartoon of Father Christmas with a little boy by his side. Santa was telling the story of Jesus' birth, and the boy inquisitively asked, 'And how did it all end?' Behind the two of them was hanging an ornamental cross. The Saviour, Jesus, was born to suffer by taking our sins on the cross.

It is a blow to our pride to realise that we are not good enough for God, and are making a mess of our world. It is painful to recognise that we need forgiveness and a new start. But that is why Jesus was born in Bethlehem. The actress Mae West got it right when she said, 'I used to be Snow White, but I drifted'. We have all drifted. Sin is something that God, who is holy, has never been able to treat lightly. It is serious. It cuts us off from God, and should keep us out of heaven and condemn us to hell. Yet Jesus came from heaven to rescue us.

Jesus, 'the Light of the World', gazed on the world's darkness; Jesus, the 'Prince of Peace', gazed on the world's wars and conflict; Jesus, who is Love, gazed on the world's hatred; Jesus came to our world to shine, to give rest and to bring life and love. As the Bible puts it: 'The Word became flesh and made his dwelling among us.'[34]

Elsewhere the Bible says, 'Here is a trustworthy saying that deserves full acceptance: Christ Jesus came into the world to save sinners'.[35]

# GET YOURSELF READY
# FOR CHRISTMAS

*O Holy Child of Bethlehem*

*Descend to us we pray;*

*Cast out our sin, and enter in,*

*Be born in us today.*

*We hear the Christmas angels*

*The great glad tidings tell:*

*O come to us, abide with us*

*Our Lord Immanuel.*

Phillips Brooks [36]

Irving Berlin stayed up all night writing the lyrics for 'White Christmas', then in the morning went to his office and told his musical secretary, 'Grab your pen and take down this song. I just wrote the best song I've ever written'. Bing Crosby introduced the song in 1941, and since then it has sold in excess of 150 million copies, recorded by well over 100 artists and bands. Bing Crosby's recording alone sold over 100 million copies. Living in Britain, I have known more white Easters than white Christmases, even though it only takes one flake of snow to fall on Christmas Day for the Met Office to regard it as a white Christmas! It may be sentimental, but virgin snow is beautiful and pure.

Hundreds of years before Jesus was born, snow features in a Bible prophecy. God appealed to His people:

> Come now, let us reason together ... Though your sins are like scarlet, they shall be as white as snow; though they are red as crimson, they shall be like wool.[37]

Our sin is being likened to huge red stains, but there is the promise that all the wrong in our lives can be completely covered and made clean again. For me that is a dream come true!

There is a Russian legend of a medieval prince, Alexis, who lived in his beautiful palace, while all around peasants lived in filthy hovels. The prince was moved by their plight and wanted to help them. He visited them and they respected him, but he never really won their confident affection.

One day a very different man came among them. He was a rough-and-ready young doctor. He rented a filthy, rat-ridden shack in one of their back streets. He wore the plainest of clothes, treated people without charge and gave away his medicines. He won their respect and affection in a way that Prince Alexis had never done.

No one ever guessed that this young doctor was in fact the prince himself, who had abandoned his palace and gone down among his people to become one of them. In a much greater way Christ stooped down to this earth from all the glory which was His in heaven. Born and lying asleep in a manger, the baby Jesus entered our world. As we have seen, the first Christmas was all about God coming into our world to deal with our separation from Him, and to make us pure in the sight of God

Himself. What does that mean for us today as we approach Christmas?

## God invites us to reason with Him

As we saw in the verses from Isaiah, God says, 'Come now, let us reason together … ' Sadly, there are people who hate God and who use their reasoning powers to show their hatred. But for those of us who are honest enough to acknowledge that this world did not happen by accident, our Maker is willing to reason with us.

God will show us that no matter how much we try, we are not the people He wants us to be. Reading newspaper headlines, as well as looking at our own lives, reminds us of that. We all know that we are not as good as we should or would like to be. We are certainly not the people God created us to be.

But God demonstrated His great love towards us in that while we were still sinners, Jesus came down from heaven to earth to go to the terrible death of crucifixion to pay for our sin. Jesus died for us – for you and me!

## God invites us to be real about ourselves

In His words from Isaiah God continues, 'Though

your sins are like scarlet ... though they are red as crimson ... ' None of us likes to think of ourselves as bad, let alone having 'scarlet', 'crimson' stains on our lives. But not one of us would even dare to look on God with the sins which dominate our thoughts, words and deeds. God is purer than the driven snow. Yet, like a sick patient being visited by a doctor, or like someone deep in debt going cap in hand to their creditor, we may go to God for a new life. He will give this to anyone who turns from their own way to trust in Him.

Jesus was called 'Wonderful Counsellor'. He really does care for us, and can cope with us. He understands us better than we understand ourselves. He knows us and is able to diagnose the issues of our life. He has the right prescription for life's pressures and sorrows. As the American writer Warren Wiersbe says, 'You and I need spiritual counsel, and Jesus Christ is perfectly qualified to be our Counsellor.'

## God invites us to receive His forgiveness

God then adds, ' ... they shall be as white as snow ... they shall be like wool.' Jesus is the Saviour. His birth in Bethlehem, His death on the cross and His rising again were all so that we might be forgiven. He came to save His people from their sins. No matter how 'scarlet' or 'red as crimson' our wrong may have been, if we ask Him to do so, God will wipe it all away, making us 'as white as snow'.

My science teacher told me that if you look at a red object through red glass, the object appears white. It never quite worked for me! But God is willing to look at us, with all our sins, through the blood of Jesus, which came from Him on the cross where He died, and see us as forgiven and pure.

Christmas may be a time of dreaming and, once in a while, of snow. It is certainly a time of giving and receiving. God has given Himself to us in Jesus. This gift was not only in a crib at Christmas, but also on a cross at Easter.

Will you receive the indescribable gift of Jesus, of forgiveness, of being made right in the sight of God, and then of heaven? The Bible teaches that heaven is not a reward, but a gift. Will you turn from your sin and trust Jesus as your Lord, Saviour and constant Companion?

## God invites us to experience true joy

Here is an insightful fact: the word 'joy' is found in the Bible 165 times. A large proportion of the message of the Bible is a very joyful one, and that is why so many people find help, hope and peace when reading the Bible, which is God's message to us.

The birth of Jesus was the opening chapter of the greatest act of rescue in the history of our world. No wonder Christmas is such a joyful event. There is joy to the world for the Lord has come.

There is much in our world to depress us: wars; injustice; tension at every level of society; starvation and famine; discredited politicians; the repeated threat of terrorism in our cities; knife crime on our streets; the binge culture; family breakdown; recession and redundancy; as well as our own sins and failures. Many of us feel deeply worried and perplexed about what is going on in the Middle East and Africa, and spilling over into Europe and the West. So can there really be joy in our complicated world? The problems that are happening today are hardly a new phenomena. We can picture the horror that arose in Bethlehem from King Herod's act of terrorism in ordering the boys under the age of two in the region to be put to death. His motive was to destroy Jesus, but one can only imagine the horrific scenes of toddlers and babies being torn from their parents and brutally killed. Yet then like now there can be peace and joy when we live in a world stained by evil.

How is this possible? The answer is found in knowing a personal relationship with God. There was no room for Jesus in the inn in Bethlehem. He was wrapped in cloths and laid simply in a manger. But as the angels said to shepherds on the hills,

> *Do not be afraid, for behold, I bring you good tidings of great joy which will be to all people. For there is born to you this day in the city of David a Saviour, who is Christ the Lord.*[38]

Lasting joy does not come from winning either the lottery, *Britain's Got Talent*, or even the Ashes or World Cup! It does not come from becoming a sports, fashion or Hollywood celebrity. Joy is not just temporary happiness. It is deep-seated and everlasting because it stems from knowing God. It can be experienced even when all around seems joyless. The glad tidings are that this great joy is offered to everyone.

Both Jewish shepherds and Gentile Arabs, the Magi with gifts, came to adore the Christ Child in

Bethlehem. Men and women were prominent throughout Jesus' ministry. Jesus was born to give joy to all people, but it is those who turn to Him who find this joy. Jesus has paid the price of our sin. He took on Himself that which cuts us off from God, and from the joy of knowing Him. Jesus took on Himself the sin of the oppressor and the oppressed; of sinners and saints; of people of the past, the present and the future.

Interestingly, near the beginning of both the Gospels of Matthew and Luke we are given the genealogy of Jesus, one through Mary's ancestral line and the other through Joseph's. One does not have to employ the researchers of the television programr *Who Do You Think You Are?* to realise the amazing ancestry of Jesus. He came through the royal line of David, so there were several male kings among His ancestors. But also listed in Matthew's genealogy is the mother of King Solomon, Bathsheba, who was originally married to a Gentile. Before her are listed Ruth and Rahab, who were also both Gentile ancestors of Jesus: one was quite saintly, the other a prostitute. They were all part of God's plan and illustrate together that Jesus, who has such a mixed human ancestry, came for all types of people. The people listed reflect us.

A year or two ago a woman in Colorado, in the United States, was rescued from drowning in the torrent of a river by a man lowered in a harness from a crane. One newspaper headlined the story 'Saviour from on high'. That is really what Jesus is! Trusting Him as your Saviour will transform your life:

- There is joy when you know that all your sin is forgiven.

- There is joy when you know that the risen, living Jesus is your Lord, Saviour and Friend.

- There is peace when you know God with you every moment of each day.

- There is peace when you know that you belong to God and are part of God's family forever.

- There is hope when you know that death is not the end, and that you need not fear being lost in eternity because one day you will go to be with God for ever in heaven.

This joy, peace and hope can be yours. Jesus, the

friend of sinners, is only a prayer away from you. In prayer, ask Him to become your Lord and Saviour, washing away all that is wrong in your life, and helping you to live as He would want you to do. Only then will you be really ready for Christmas!

# NOTES

## Introduction

1. Genesis 3:15.

2. For these Old Testament prophecies, see Isaiah 7:14; Psalm 2:7; Isaiah 9:6; Micah 5:2 and Hosea 11:1.

3. Luke 2:11, NKJV.

4. Matthew 2:1–2.

## 1. Christmas is special – get ready!

5. From the carol 'O Holy Night'.

6. Luke 2:10–11.

7. Luke 2:14.

8    Matthew 2:16.

9    1 John 4:14, NKJV.


## 2. God prepared the world for the first Christmas

10   From the carol 'It Came Upon the
     Midnight Clear'.

11   Genesis 3:15.

12   For these prophecies, see Micah 5:2; Isaiah
     7:14; Matthew 2:23; Hosea 11:1.

13   Psalm 22 and Isaiah 53.

14   Luke 2:10–11 and 13–14, NKJV.

15   Isaiah 57:20–21.

16   These incidents can be found in John 19:26–
     27; Luke 23:46; John 14:27.

17   Isaiah 2:4.


## 3. God came down at Christmas

18   From the carol 'Once in Royal David's City'.

19   John 1:6.

20   See John 1:1 and Genesis 1:1.

21 You can hear this recording by going to: www.youtube.com/watch?v=njpWalYduU4

22 Luke 2:1–5.

23 Isaiah 9:6–7, NKJV.

24 John 1:1 and 14.

25 Colossians 1:15, NKJV.

26 John 10:17–18, NKJV.

## 4. God, making us ready for Him

27 From the carol 'See, Amid the Winter's Snow'.

28 Betrothal in Bible days was a step beyond engagement, which involved deeper commitment but not yet the union of marriage.

29 John 4:1–26 and 29, NKJV.

30 Luke 19:1–10.

31 John 8:1–11, NKJV.

32 Luke 23:42–43, NKJV.

33 John 3:16, NKJV.

34 John 1:14.

35 1 Timothy 1:15.

## 5. Get yourself ready for Christmas

36   From the carol 'O Little Town of Bethlehem'.

37   Isaiah 1:18.

38   Luke 2:10–11, NKJV.

a division of **10**of**those**.com

**10Publishing** is the publishing house of **10ofThose**.
It is committed to producing quality Christian
resources that are biblical and accessible.

**www.10ofthose.com** is our online retail arm selling
thousands of quality books at discounted prices.

For information contact: **info@10ofthose.com**
or check out our website: **www.10ofthose.com**